JON

and

JORDAN KNIGHT

of the

NEW KIDS ON THE BLOCK

By Maria Rainer

Modern Publishing
A Division of Unisystems, Inc.
New York, New York 10022

Book Design by Bob Feldgus

Printed in the U.S.A.

CONTENTS

Both Jon and Jordan credit their church choirmaster for teaching them "almost everything they know" about music. Janet Macoska

INTRODUCTION

When "Please Don't Go Girl" from the *Hangin' Tough* album started climbing the charts, who would have known what was to come? If anyone told Jonathan Knight, Jordan Knight, Donald Wahlberg, Daniel Wood and Joseph McIntyre that all of their dreams would shortly be coming true, they would never have believed it!

After "Please Don't Go Girl" became a hit, four more hits followed. These five Boston lads were breaking records left and right. Suddenly, teen gals across America were singing "You got the right stuff, baby," along with Donnie on their Walkmans, stadiums were selling out date after date, and record stores couldn't keep up with the demand for the New Kids' *Hangin' Tough* album. Columbia Records shipped over two million copies of the New Kids' latest album, *Step By Step,* to record stores around the country for Tuesday, June 5, 1990's on-sale date. By Wednesday, June 6, re-orders brought album sales up to three million. The sales figures for the "Step By Step" home video followed a similar path.

The New Kids On The Block are a phenomenal success! Their funky pop music makes teen girls dance and scream. The reactions the New Kids evoke and the huge crowds they draw have been compared more than once to Beatlemania. Who are these kids and what's their story?

This book will go back to the late '60s, beginning with the births of Jonathan Rashleigh Knight and Jordan Nathaniel Marcel Knight, two members of New Kids On The Block. Learn lots of personal stuff about adorable brothers Jonathan and Jordan ranging from their school days to afternoon rehearsals to their prosperous days as New Kids!

Find out vital data about each brother from the type of girls they like to their secret dreams. Chock full of facts, stats, and juicy tidbits, you won't want to miss this story about America's most popular band today!

Though Jon daydreamed of being famous, it was Jordan who constantly walked through the house singing. Chris Mackie

1

THE WAY IT WAS

IN THE BEGINNING

The date was November 29, 1968 in Worcester, Massachusetts when the sweet little cries of hazel-eyed Jonathan Rashleigh Knight pierced the air. Mom, Marlene, and dad, Allan, were delighted to bring this bundle of joy into their home in nearby Lancaster. Jonathan joined his four siblings Allison, Sharon, David and Christopher. From the beginning, Allison and Sharon were always more than happy to lend their mother a helping hand with the new baby. Jonathan's middle name was in honor of his paternal grandmother's maiden name.

Marlene remembers that Jonathan was very quiet, tender and affectionate. "He would tug on your skirt and whisper to get your attention," she remembers. "But once he had your attention, he would never shut up! He'd chat and talk and laugh—but he was very quiet about getting your attention and that is still true!"

Eighteen months later, on May 17, 1970, Jordan Nathaniel Marcel Knight was born in the same hospital in

Worcester as his brother. Marlene chose to name her sixth child "Jordan" after the River Jordan from the Bible. Marlene's family, the Putmans, are from Canada and she also wanted to select names that represented the English and the French. Jordan was a dreamy little chubby-cheeked kid, and his big brown eyes were always smiling. It's no wonder that Marlene has always described Jordan as her "enchanted one."

Sister Sharon remembers how she and the other Knight kids received the news of Jordan's birth. The boys didn't seem to mind that there would be another boy in the family, but the girls sure did—at first anyway! Sharon was six and Allison was seven. Their father called them into his room and told them their mom had just had a baby boy. "Allison and I were so upset that we started crying because we already had three boys in the family and we wanted a sister!" recalls Sharon. "But we got little Jordan instead and he was really cute. So, we got over our sadness quickly!"

After spending a brief period in Lancaster, the Knights moved to a Boston suburb called Westwood. Jon and Jordan were always extremely close to one another, and did almost everything together. They shared a room, played together and they eventually went to the same schools.

Both Marlene and Allan's families are from Ontario, Canada, so Jordan, Jon and the rest of the Knight gang often traveled up to Canada to visit. The kids really loved to pile into the family station wagon and go to their grandparents' cottage every summer. All of the relatives would gather there, so it was a time when the Knight children saw their cousins and other relatives. Spending time together with family was very important to Marlene and Allan—a value they passed on to their children. Today, now that Jon and Jordan are so famous, family togetherness is more important than ever!

Although the Knight family did not live in poverty, it was sometimes hard to make ends meet. Allan was a carpenter by trade, but later became an Episcopal minister, and after Marlene graduated from college, she became a social worker and specialized in family therapy. When they finally could afford to move, the Knights bought a huge Victorian house in Dorchester, a Boston suburb. There was much more room in this house. In fact, before the Knights moved in, there were three different families living there! Though the extra space was welcome, there was also plenty of hard work in store for everyone!

Jordan Nathaniel Marcel Knight first joined the rest of his family on May 17, 1970. Janet Macoska

SETTLING DOWN AND GROWING UP

The Knights' new house had ten bedrooms and four bathrooms. The kids loved roaming from room to room and so did the various pets that were also part of the family. When the Knights moved in, they had plenty of repairs to make to get the house into better shape. As you probably can imagine, a big house needs to be constantly maintained and the Knights' immense lawn always seemed to need mowing. With plenty of kids to help, though, it was not too much of a burden on Marlene or Allan.

Everyone was expected to pitch in, run errands and do their chores. "We had this board which listed all of our names and underneath the names were our chores for the week and the day we were supposed to do them," recalls Allison. And Jon and Jordan weren't excluded from doing the dishes or laundry just because they were boys. Jon adored working outside in the garden, as did his sister, Sharon. Even now, when Jon comes home from touring with the New Kids, he spends quite a bit of his spare time in the yard planting trees and flowers and making repairs around the house.

Aside from the usual squabbles, the Knight kids got along pretty well for such a large family. Jon and Jordan both played hockey when they were very young; and Jordan also played soccer. These new kids on the block fit right into the neighborhood. The street the Knights lived on was filled with big families with lots of kids. So, if a brother or sister was busy, Jordan and Jon could always find some neighborhood playmates to play stick ball, tag or street basketball. How about a go-cart race? That was pretty fun for all the kids, too! Sometimes, the neighborhood children would get together and have a block party of sorts by opening up a fire hydrant and creating their own "Jet-pool." Jordan and Jon loved slipping into their swim trunks and leaping through the stream of water to cool off on hot summer days. And since the block that the Knights lived on sloped, it was ideal for sledding in the winter months. The Knight kids would hop on a toboggan and enjoy the ride.

Although the Knights' old Victorian house had seventeen rooms, Jon and Jordan still shared a room. Why, you ask? It was because their mom had a big, generous heart, and literally took her work home with her. As a social worker, she specialized in family therapy and whenever she could, she would invite foster

Jon with his favorite lady, his mom, Marlene Putman. Star File

Jordan says he learned to be caring and sensitive to the needs of others from his mom's example. Janet Macoska

children and elderly and disabled people who couldn't live on their own to stay at the Knight house. Marlene had created a program for children who were not able to live successfully in other foster homes. So, ever since Jon and Jordan can remember, there was a steady stream of people coming and going through their front door.

Jon and Jordan really didn't know much about these other children when they were young. They just knew that there was always someone around to play with and joke around with. But as Jordan and Jon got older, Marlene explained that others were less fortunate. Jon and Jordan thought their mom was the greatest and loved her dearly. For most children, the idea of sharing doesn't always come easy. However, the Knight children were as generous as their mom, not only sharing their house, but their toys, their books, their television set, their food and their parents with their foster brothers and sisters. This plays a big part in how Jordan and Jon treat others today.

All of the kids would play together in the large backyard. Sometimes they'd put on dances and little plays together. In fact, Jon and Jordan started performing in plays at a very young age. One of Marlene's fondest memories is when four-year-old Jordan played baby Jesus in a school Christmas play.

Both Jordan and Jon agree that they remember being a little frustrated at times with all of the bustling activity that was going on in the house. Privacy was not something that came easily with all of the people running in and out of the house. Although the kids were never jealous of the foster children, they did feel crowded at times. Despite that fact, the Knight children grew close to many of the foster kids who stayed with them, and were very proud of what their mother was doing. They also were thrilled that everyone thought of their home as full of excitement and energy.

Aside from celebrating birthdays in a special way, another thing you could count on all the Knights to participate in was attending church. Since Allan was a minister, religion and music had a prominent place in all the Knights' lives. Allan played guitar and Marlene played the accordion. The kids really loved to watch The Donnie and Marie Osmond Show. With such a keen interest in church and music, it was inevitable that the Knight children would join the All Saints Episcopal Church Choir.

Jordan and Jon really loved singing in the choir. When you ask them about musical influences, they almost always mention the positive influence that singing in their church choir had on them early on in their lives. Jordan had such an amazing voice that he was often a soloist. At first, he was terrified to sing solo. But, eventually, he got over his stage fright and would really belt it out. Of course, having the whole Knight family there applauding and giving support was always a great comfort to both Jon and Jordan. Sisters Sharon and Allison also sang in the choir. Rehearsals were twice a week and the choir sang on Sundays. In the summer, Jon and Jordan went off to church camp and had plenty of fun singing, swimming and just being kids!

Jon and Jordan sure did love to perform. According to Jon, Jordan would walk around the house singing and he still does it today. And though Jordan loved to sing, he really never planned on being a professional singer. Surprisingly enough, it was Jon who daydreamed about being famous. At the time, who would have thought the names Jon and Jordan Knight would soon be thrilling teen girls' hearts all across the globe?

OFF TO SCHOOL

Education was very important to Marlene, and the Knight children were always encouraged to learn and grow from the people and experiences around them. At the time Jon and Jordan were entering elementary school, busing was being used as a means for integrating the black and white areas of Boston. Jordan and Jon both were bused to William Monroe Trotter Elementary School in Roxbury, which is about a half-hour ride from where the Knights lived in Dorchester. Jordan and Jon used this experience to make friends with many different kids. Making friends was no problem at all for adorable Jon and Jordan. Because of their open and accepting personalities, they were always very popular.

Also riding the bus to Trotter were two boys named Donnie Wahlberg and Danny Wood. Ring a bell? The boys eventually met and became friendly. Ironically, although all four auditioned for the school chorus, Donnie, the first member of NKOTB, was not selected.

As many little boys do, Jon and Jordan got into some minor clashes. "I had a couple when I was young," recalls Jon. "The last one I got into was when I was eight. It was after school and this kid tried to cut through my yard to get to his house. I told him he'd have to go around the block to get to it, then I just picked him up and threw him out."

Jon and Jordan were very enthusiastic about school and did really well. After elementary school, they enrolled in Phyllis Wheatley Middle School where pals Danny and Donnie were also going. However, Jon and Jordan won scholarships to Thayer Academy, a private school in Braintree, a suburb of Boston. Since they had to take the train to Thayer, they learned how to use public transportation at an early age. That meant they didn't have to ask mom and dad for a ride every time they wanted to go to the mall or to a movie. Instead, they just looked on a "T" map and took the appropriate line to where they wanted to go. They bid their public school pals good-bye and started commuting to Thayer on the "T," Boston's subway system.

Life at the Thayer Academy Middle School was pretty different from what Jon and Jordan were used to. When the two brothers arrived, most of the suburban kids were in awe of them. The main reason was because Jon and Jordan were city kids and dressed differently, and their classmates thought that the differences were cool. Of course, there were some kids who were uncomfortable around Jordan and Jon, basing their feelings on incorrect stereotypes about city kids liking to fight. Though popular, Jon and Jordan missed their old friends, and at first it was difficult for them to adjust to their new school.

As in any school, there were cliques, and Jon and Jordan were considered part of the "popular" group. Once the other kids got to know the Knight brothers, they knew that they were just two caring, intelligent and handsome boys. Jordan joined the school's basketball team, while Jon spent much of his after-school time back in Dorchester hanging out with his neighborhood buddies. The Knight brothers became well known at Thayer not only for their great looks, but also for their gentle and approachable natures. One classmate of theirs told a teen magazine that even way back then, Jon and Jordan were very popular with the girls.

In late 1982, *Thriller* was released and Michael Jackson fever was spreading. A big part of the Michael Jackson craze was the fascination with his unique street-inspired dancing. A classmate of Jordan's told a teen magazine that Jordan used to Moonwalk in the

Jon is sure to have a future career in management because he is so calm, efficient, and well-organized. Janet Macoska

hallways and do some excellent M.J. impersonations. Everyone was enthralled with the younger Knight brother's exceptional dance moves. Jordan's great admiration for Michael Jackson led him to try to dance and even dress like him. And this was only the beginning. In the upcoming chapters you'll see how Jordan grew more and more fond of music and dancing.

It is not surprising at all that Jordan went to many school dances. As expected, he was a huge hit. He would Moonwalk and execute his fancy footwork with the greatest dexterity. In class the next day, the buzz would be pretty loud about how great Jordan danced at last night's dance. If you've ever seen a New

Kids' concert, you know that Jordan is very light on his feet. It's fascinating to think that many of his amazing dance moves come naturally to this New Kid.

When Jon graduated from the eighth grade, his class voted him the "Most Flirtatious!" It's pretty surprising to think that was the case since, today, Jon is usually described as being the shy New Kid. Although many magazines and fans think that Jon is extremely shy, that's not the case at all. Jon was admired by many of the other guys in the school, because he always was in the company of girls. "Jonathan is always thought of as the quiet member of the group, but if you're around him all the time, forget it—he's as wild as the rest of us—especially after a long night on the tour bus!" explains Jordan.

Jon doesn't really think "shy" is a good adjective to describe his personality. Friends describe him as the type of person who likes small groups and one-on-one conversations. "People think he is shy because he is always in the back on stage," says one close friend. "He does not have to have a spotlight." So, it fits that Jon wouldn't exactly be thrilled about giving an oral report or a speech in class, but he loved making new friends or talking and hanging out with his old pals.

Another secret from Jon and Jordan's past is that in the 1983 Thayer Yearbook, Jon left a very special and amusing message for his brother in his Last Will and Testament. In the yearbook's Class Will, the message reads: "I, Jon Knight, leave my flirtatious skills to my brother Jordan."

After Jon graduated from the eighth grade, the Knight brothers left Thayer and enrolled in a public high school called English High. Jordan and Jon were really happy to get back into public school because they felt that they had the chance to meet kids of all different cultures and nationalities there rather than in a private school. The city was a place that the Knight brothers found very nurturing in terms of excitement.

Mom Marlene let all of her children have a certain amount of independence—as long as all of their chores were done and they obeyed the general Knight household rules. It was during their high school years that Jon and Jordan were in for a few surprises.

After Jordan became a member of Maurice Starr's new group, he had to convince Jon to audition. Larry Busacca/Retna

CHANGES

During their teen years, Jon and Jordan went through some major transitions. Jordan was spending more and more time hanging out with his pals on the streets. He liked going to parties, dancing and staying out late. For a while, Jordan and his friends were writing their name or "tag" on the Boston subway cars—something a lot of city kids did (and still do) for fun. Fortunately, Jordan turned his talents and energy away from this destructive expression of creativity before he got into trouble. Although many people think that the term "street kids" means trouble in the sense of gangs and such, that was not the case with the Knight brothers at all.

Jon, on the other hand, never went through a similar phase. Jon liked to feel independent, and, therefore, it was important to him to work and earn his own money. Ever since he was younger, Jon had been ambitious and hard-working—and he's had the jobs to prove it! "I had about twelve jobs," he laughs. "I used to be a clerk. I used to be a head chef in a restaurant. I worked in a Burger King. And I used to look after disabled kids." As you can imagine, Jon was quite busy as a teen, working and going to school.

When Jon was about fifteen, his parents decided to divorce. It's a topic that neither brother really likes to discuss with the press. They have both indicated in past interviews that it is a subject that is extremely personal to them, and is not something that should be laid bare in the public spotlight for all to see. They also feel that there are many children whose parents are divorced and that it really shouldn't be such a big deal to everyone. In any case, Marlene and Allan went their separate ways, and it was a difficult time for the entire Knight family. As you know, family togetherness was greatly emphasized as Jon and Jordan were growing up, so when the news came that their parents were splitting up, they were very confused and hurt.

The fact that Marlene's specialty was family therapy was a big help. She always encouraged her kids to communicate and talk about their problems. Some parents are so distant that it is almost impossible for their children to even admit they have a problem. The Knight kids, though, learned at a young age that everyone has problems. Honesty and openness were stressed in the Knight family. Jordan and Jon's sister Sharon says that they have their parents to thank for their good qualities. They instilled good, basic values in all of their children and always talked to the kids when they misbehaved instead of just punishing them. They would sit them down and discuss what the child needed to do to improve his or her behavior. And the foster kids were not exempt from these serious discussions.

Slowly, Marlene and her children adjusted to the divorce. The Knight kids and the foster children were very supportive of Marlene because they understood the pressure she was under. The most important thing at that crucial time was that everyone stuck together. Jon got more involved with working because he felt that he should be helping his mom by taking care of himself more and being more financially independent. Even at such a young age, Jon took responsibility for himself. Today, it is easy to understand why Jon is the practical New Kid who makes sure the other New Kids are doing what they're supposed to be doing, and that things are going according to plan.

During the time of his parents' divorce, Jordan was being drawn more and more toward dancing. He spent a lot of his free time with his pals who were absolutely crazy about breakdancing, an especially popular pastime in urban areas.

Jordan would watch his black friends' stylish moves

and he would pick up the steps in no time at all. Jordan would also practice breaking and body-popping with his pal, Danny Wood, on street corners and in school yards. They would spend many afternoons just talking about all the songs and musicians they liked. Jordan would practice at home and make up some hip moves himself and then teach his friends. In fact, Jordan and Danny even got jobs as camp counselors one summer, teaching kids how to breakdance. They both enjoyed working with the younger kids and remember that whole summer as being barrels of fun. Anyone who has seen a New Kids' concert has to believe that Jordan and Danny both have dancing in their blood!

While Jon was engrossed in his job and Jordan was drawn to music and dancing, there was a musical project brewing in Boston. If someone had told the boys that they would be performing in stadiums across the world drawing megacrowds of screaming fans in a few years, Jordan never would have believed it. Dancing and singing to Jordan were just outlets for his creativity. He never really thought about becoming famous because it never really interested him. Performing was just something Jordan liked to do. Jon, however, was a different story. As a teenager, Jon was the one who used to fantasize about being a huge pop star someday. "I used to sit in front of the mirror and sing, dreaming about making it big, doubting I would," says Jon. Little did Jon know that his dream would be coming true in just a few years!

SUMMER OF '84

Somewhere in Dorchester, Donald Wahlberg was rapping and breakdancing his little heart out. He loved the funky music and he enjoyed winging raps out on-the-spot with his pals. One day a neighborhood pal told him that there was a woman conducting a talent search for five cute and talented young guys. Donnie thought about auditioning, but he just kept putting it off. After his friend kept telling him to check it out, Donnie decided to give it a go one day. The woman's name was Mary Alford and she was a talent manager (and personnel officer at the Massachusetts Department of Education) from Dorchester. She met Donnie and told him that the boys that she was looking for needn't be incredible singers or incredibly gorgeous for that matter. They did, though, have to have character and the ability to catch on quickly. She then took Donnie and his little brother, Mark, to Roxbury. That's where the man forming the band lived.

The man with the "idea" was Maurice Starr, the famous record producer who propelled Roxbury's New Edition (the launching pad for Bobby Brown's highly successful singing career) into the limelight. Donnie just tried to be himself. When Maurice asked him, "What do you do?" Donnie told him that he could rap and breakdance. After Maurice heard Donnie's fresh raps and watched his slick breaking moves, he told him he was in the group. After that, Mark auditioned and he got in, too! Then Maurice told the two brothers about his plans for the musical project he was developing. Donnie was awestruck as Maurice gushed about how this band of his was going to be so popular and about how there would be chart-topping tunes, and so on. Maurice was so enthusiastic and optimistic that it

Admired by thousands, Jordan uses his popularity to encourage young people to stay in school and to say "No" to drugs.
Vinnie Zuffante, Star File

would have been odd if some of his sassy confidence *didn't* rub off on Donnie. When Donnie and Mark left Maurice's home, they had stars in their eyes. Donnie, especially, was really pumped up about what the future had in store for him!

Mary told Donnie that if he knew of any boys that would be good for the band, then he should tell them to audition for Maurice. Donnie told her that he would tell his friends. One of the first names that popped into Donnie's head was Danny Wood. He called Danny and excitedly told him all about Maurice and the band. Incredibly, Danny said that he was not interested. Donnie would bug Danny everyday about auditioning, but Danny said he was in a breakdancing group called

Rock Against Racism and he didn't want to give that up. In the meantime, Mark lost interest. He was more into just being a kid and hanging out with his friends. "He was into basketball then," Mary told a Boston magazine recently.

One warm summer day in '84, Donnie was racking his brain to find someone who would be good for the group when he suddenly remembered Jonathan and Jordan Knight from way back in elementary school. He remembered that Jordan, Jon and Danny were all in the school chorus. He had lost track of them, but he finally hunted them down and told Jordan all about the group. Jordan decided to give it a shot and off he went to Roxbury to audition for Maurice. Although Jordan was used to singing around the house and in front of people, you can bet your fave New Kids' poster that he had butterflies flitting about in his tummy. But Maurice was very warmhearted and casual, so it wasn't exactly an uptight audition. After Jordan finished singing, Maurice smiled and welcomed him into the group. You can bet Donnie was psyched when he found out the good news!

Meanwhile, Donnie had finally convinced Danny to at least audition for Maurice. So, Danny hooked up with Maurice. He rapped a bit and after an impressive audition chock-full of exhilarating breaking and body popping, Danny was accepted, too!

Jordan had gone home and told Jonathan all about the band. Jonathan was thrilled for Jordan, but he wasn't so sure if he wanted to try out. "I didn't want to try out because I didn't think I could sing and dance and rap," admits Jon. He's the type of guy who doesn't like to be shoved into the limelight, so Jordan had to coax him into trying out. He told Jon that he didn't have to be the world's best singer or dancer, and that Maurice was more concerned with an "interesting look" and personality. Finally, Jon decided to audition for Maurice. And, naturally, he passed with flying colors!

The fifth member was a kid named Jamie Kelley, a friend of Donnie's. All of the members were about the same age. A little while after Mark dropped out, Jamie decided to leave as well. He was pressured by his parents somewhat, but he decided, like Mark, that he missed being a regular kid. The band rehearsals were tough on all the guys. Mary used to pick them up every day after school and they rehearsed until about nine at night. When Jamie decided to leave, the guys were disappointed since they were just getting comfortable with one another. Anyway, this time around, Maurice decided to stick with his original plan for the band. He wanted a band like the Osmonds but with more soul. ''I wanted a white New Edition,'' says Maurice. So, the deal was that the fifth member should be younger than Donnie, Danny, Jordan and Jon and have a high singing voice. So, the search was on—again.

It took a while, but Mary finally tracked down a twelve-year-old kid named Joseph McIntyre who, at the time, was attending St. Mary's of Assumption in Brookline, another suburb of Boston. Joe lived (and still does) in Jamaica Plain and had been involved with neighborhood theater groups (along with his sisters) since he was six years old. So, the townsfolk were somewhat acquainted with the McIntyre name. When Mary told people she was looking for a young sweet-looking boy to join a band, everyone thought of adorable Joseph McIntyre. Mary finally found Joe and told him all about Maurice's musical project. Back then, Joe had straight hair and wore braces. And he sure was tiny compared to the other guys. He obviously had not experienced his growth spurt! Anyway, he auditioned and Maurice was extremely pleased with his high, sweet voice. Ultimately, a band was born!

Jordan, devoted to music, spends his free time studying the keyboards, writing songs, and developing musical projects.

Janet Macoska

MAKING IT HAPPEN

As far as family support goes, the Knights, Wahlbergs, Woods and McIntyres are 400 percent behind the boys! However, that wasn't always the case. As each guy went home and told his family about Maurice's project, they got similar reactions—skepticism, distrust and disbelief. If you think about it, it was a natural reaction. Who was this man? Was he telling the truth? Why was he so sure their sons were going to become so famous? All these questions and more needed to be answered—or at least discussed—before the boys' parents would let them officially join the band.

So, Jon and Jordan's mother, Marlene, started to check things out. Jordan had told her that Maurice Starr produced New Edition. First, she verified that, and then she did some more checking up on Maurice's background. She met Maurice and they had a long talk about Jon and Jordan's future. He impressed her with his optimism, just as he had dazzled Alma Conroy, Donnie's mother. He had high hopes for the boys and he was definite about the future. Maurice never said ''*if* the band is successful.'' He talked about success as if it were a fact—as if he had a crystal ball and he could see into the future. After meeting Maurice, Marlene agreed to let Jordan and Jon join. Joe's parents felt good about the group and knew that he wanted to be in show business, so they also gave him their blessings. Although Danny's parents, Elizabeth (Betty) and Daniel, Sr., at first were against the whole idea, they left the decision to Danny. However, it was very important to the Woods that Danny get a good education, and he had just received a full scholarship to Boston University. So, Danny decided to attend school and stay in the band. (He would later put college on hold.)

In the beginning, Jordan, Jon, Danny and Donnie did not readily accept Joe. Joe wasn't from Dorchester, he was younger and smaller, and he dressed differently. Similarly, Joe wasn't exactly thrilled to be away from all of his pals from Jamaica Plain. So, in the early stages of the band, there were the guys—and then there was Joe.

After they started rehearsing together, the guys started to get to know Joe little by little. He was a sweet and energetic kid, who eventually found his way straight to their hearts. Although the guys still picked on him occasionally, it was more of a "little brother" thing. So, Jon, Jordan, Danny, Donnie and Joe were becoming like family!

And it's a good thing because they rehearsed everyday with Maurice and Mary. Often, the boys practiced in Jordan and Jon's basement. Their sister, Sharon, admits that at times it used to drive her up the wall, but deep down, she always knew that there was something special about the band, and that they were going to be successful. Whenever they had the time, Marlene and the rest of the Knights used to sit in and watch the guys in action as did the other guys' family members. The guys were never shy about having their families there watching them. In fact, they liked it that they had an audience to test their routines on. In Jordan and Jon's case, with the addition of all their foster brothers and sisters, they had a healthy-sized group of supporters even from the start!

Marlene says that in the early days of the band, she felt sad that Jon and Jordan always had to rehearse. "I felt so sorry for them when their friends would be out working part-time jobs and making money to go out on dates and have fun, and they would be down in the basement rehearsing." Although she felt that the boys were missing "the best years of their lives," she supported and respected their decision to give the group a

Jon with his friend Dino, a former Las Vegas deejay who toured with the New Kids last winter. Janet Macoska

chance.

The name that Maurice gave the band was "Nynuk." He roughly defines it as meaning "love throughout the nations." Well, the name was not exactly the most popular with the guys, but they stuck with it for a while. Their first show was at the Joseph Lee School in Dorchester. Jordan, Jon, Donnie, Danny and Joe lip-synced the show. Maurice recorded the music (he played most of the instruments onto a tape) and the guys just sang along and danced. In those days, Nynuk's audience was mostly black. The guys were booed on more than one occasion, but eventually they received a more positive reception.

After receiving negative feedback about the name "Nynuk," Maurice agreed to change it to something else. "New Kids On The Block," the title of a funky song from their first album, became their new name. They shopped around for a record deal and eventually settled on Columbia Records. Their debut album was called *New Kids On The Block* and was released in April of 1986. The album featured an adorable shot of the youthful Kids on the cover.

Although everyone had high hopes, the album didn't do much on the charts at all—in the beginning that is. The first single, "Be My Girl," got some airplay on Boston stations. The first time Jon and Jordan's sister, Sharon, heard the song on the radio, she was with Jon at the beach. "I was like 'Jonathan! There's your song! It's on the radio!'" she recalls. But Jon was very subdued about the whole thing because nothing much was happening with the group at the time. Still, every time "Be My Girl" was on the radio, the Knight family turned up the volume!

In March of 1988, the New Kids released *Hangin' Tough,* and almost immediately after its release, the New Kids got a break from pop radio. A station disc jockey in Tampa, Florida liked the song "Please Don't

Go Girl'' and started playing it on the air. Other stations followed suit and soon, New Kids' fans started to multiply.

The group got its biggest break when they hooked up with Tiffany's booking agent. He agreed to try to book the New Kids On the Block as her opening act. Well, Tiffany agreed to see the Kids, so they filed into her dressing room one day, interrupting the pop star's lunch. They did their routine in the confines of an extremely small dressing room, and Tiffany, to say the least, was so impressed that she agreed to let the Kids open for her national tour. Jon is convinced that if Tiffany hadn't given them that break so long ago, the Kids may very well still be struggling to this day.

After touring with Tiffany, New Kids mania started to spread. The New Kids' second album went on to hatch the smash singles ''You Got It (The Right Stuff),'' ''I'll Be Lovin' You (Forever),'' ''Hangin' Tough'' and ''Cover Girl.'' The New Kids' debut album was re-released in 1989 and it went on to spawn some hits of its own! Their name was becoming extremely well-known and their popularity shot straight through the roof of Boston and exploded all over America! *Hangin' Tough* was breaking records at every turn! The New Kids embarked on their own national tour and consistently performed to sell-out stadiums. Thousands of New Kids' fans agree that a New Kids' show is a very magical experience! And so, the New Kids On The Block suddenly weren't so new anymore!

2

JONATHAN KNIGHT

SHY GUY?

Jonathan Rashleigh Knight prefers that people call him Jonathan rather than Jon, although hardly anyone does. Jordan, Donnie, Joe, Danny, his family and his friends may describe Jonathan as being the shy guy in the band, but you have to understand what that means. When the Cover Girls (one of the many bands that opened for the New Kids during their Hangin' Tough tour) were asked if Jon was shy, they all said no way! Of all the New Kids, Jon was the dude who used to go visit the Cover Girls in their dressing room and just chill with them for a bit. He liked to chat with them and just find out what they had been up to that day before the show. He may look very introverted and reserved, but Jon is very outgoing and *loves* to talk!

However, Jon isn't the type of guy who would enjoy being trapped by a mob of screaming fans. If you think about it, who would? It's really kind of scary. A situation of this type will immediately provoke Jon to withdraw. One of Jon's not-so-fond memories is when dozens of fans swarmed around a jacuzzi he was relaxing in at a hotel. "I felt like a fish in an aquarium," says Jon of the experience.

Jonathan Rashleigh Knight—soft-spoken, street-smart, and star performer.

Jon really loves to shop! The other Kids didn't nickname him "GQ" for nothing! Jon enjoys buying stylish clothes and really likes the sensational effect of mixing white and black-colored clothing. It can be a real wild scene if all the New Kids just decided to hop in a car and go shopping at the mall! So, Jon and the other guys usually end up going with their "large and in charge" security guards.

Although Marlene Knight was a little worried that the sudden fame and fortune would spoil her sons and possibly turn them into show-biz brats, she really didn't have anything to worry about. Jon and Jordan are really down-to-earth guys who aren't interested in material things. Jon loves the simple things in life. When the New Kids toured Japan, Jon spent some of his spare time feeding chickens on a farm rather than working up a sweat in a hot Tokyo disco. In fact, all of the New Kids like to just chill out with their families and friends. And, of course, they like to give their fans back some of the love and support they give them each and every day by performing and making them smile!

While Jon is onstage, he likes to let the New Kids' fans know how much he loves and cares about them! "Sometimes I'll point to someone or look straight into a fan's eyes to let them know I'm there for them," reveals this handsome New Kid.

If you happen to be in the vicinity of a New Kids' show and just happen to bump into Jon in the lobby of a hotel, he'd probably like for you to come over and say hello. But keep in mind that he doesn't like it when fans scream and cause a huge fuss. "I really like people, it's just that sometimes you're a little scared," explains Jon. "I kind of want to size someone up before I talk to them."

Now, this isn't to say that Jon doesn't like to get to know New Kids' fans. On the contrary, he loves signing autographs and just rapping with fans about themselves. In fact, all of the New Kids like to find out more personal info about their fans. So, if you happen to bump into a New Kid, don't ask them too many questions about the group. Try starting the conversation off by talking about something you might have in common. For instance, talk about the *other* bands that you like or maybe about your love of animals: Jon, for example, has always had a special place in his heart for animals. As a youngster, he had lots of pets—rats, dogs, chickens, rabbits, ducks, pigs and a pony! Even now, Jon travels with and takes care of, and dearly loves, his Shar-Pei. Although you would think that the adorable, wrinkly-skinned dog would sleep with Jon on the tour bus, that's not the case. Apparently, the pooch doesn't like heights, so he cuddles up with Jordan who sleeps on the bottom bunk on the bus. Awww, how cute!

Sometimes, Jon may be rushing out the door in order to make it on time to a sound check. In that case he'd like to stop and sign an autograph or two, but he really can't. "It really breaks our hearts if we have to say no to someone who has been supportive of us," he explains. "So sometimes, when we have to catch a plane or if we're running late getting to a rehearsal, our security guards have to pull us away!" When the New Kids are just chilling at the local mall or restaurant,

Jordan and Jon, though different in many ways, have been almost inseparable their whole lives. Janet Macoska

though, they have signed autographs on the spur of the moment on many, many occasions!

If you've seen a New Kids' concert, you know that Jon rarely takes the lead. This is because Jon prefers to have a one-on-one conversation rather than conversing with a huge group of people. As you've probably guessed by now, Jon was not exactly at ease at early New Kids performances. But he is getting more relaxed each and every day! He does duets with Jordan onstage and if you remember, Jonathan sang lead vocals for the first time on the New Kids' third album, *Merry, Merry Christmas.* That's Jon's sweet voice you hear on ''I'm Dreaming of a White Christmas!''

FAMILY AND FRIENDS

"**T**he great part of having my brother in the group is that I can always talk to him," reveals Jordan. "I think that I would go crazy if Jonathan weren't with me in the group." Naturally, Jonathan feels the same way about Jordan. Maybe it's because Jonathan is the oldest New Kid, but he always finds himself keeping the guys in line by making sure they hustle when they're running late and that they don't joke around too much when they shouldn't be.

Johnny Wright, the New Kids' announcer and production manager (he's the guy who pumps up the audiences before the Kids take the stage), says that Jon is always keeping an eye on things. "Jon's going to make a great manager because he's a detail man," says Johnny.

It seems that the New Kids On The Block have been on tour forever! The early part of this past spring was spent touring the United Kingdom (U.K.). Then the Kids returned and after a few weeks off, they kicked off their Magic Summer '90 tour in late June. Considering how hard they work and all the time they spend away from their families, it follows that they get homesick. "You can feel really far away from home and start to get homesick—and you know you can't go home for a month," says Jonathan. "That can be a real drag!" However, he is quick to add that, on the flipside, the Kids get to meet all sorts of people from different cultural backgrounds. All of the Kids think that's cool and that's why they like to travel so much!

Of course, whenever the Knight family can, they are there giving Jon and Jordan their support! You can find Marlene at almost all of the Boston and New York shows cheering for her sons. The energy of a New Kids' show is unbelievable! Everyone is so pumped up! Marlene says that when she sees Jonathan and Jordan up onstage, she just sees her sons—just two regular guys. But she can also see what all the girls are screaming about, too! There's no doubt that Marlene is a big fan of New Kids On The Block!

Jon's Shar-Pei is no longer a puppy. Todd Kaplan, Star File

THE REAL JONATHAN

Jonathan Knight is a real laid-back kind of guy. He describes himself as being "caring, sensitive and hard-working." Jon usually likes to relax by taking a swim or if the Kids are near the slopes, he likes to ski. As far as vacationing goes, Jon really loves the warm breezes and clear waters of Hawaii. He also likes Italian food, milk shakes and French fries, but you won't find him or Jordan eating backstage before a concert. If they do eat something, it may just be a bowl of cereal.

Other things that are on Jonathan's "like" list are black BMWs, science, chocolate, Hostess Cupcakes, art, love, peace, happiness, good health, the colors black and white, recording in the studio, traveling, *The Cosby Show* and girls who are independent. Jon's dislikes include being homesick, not being able to listen to his huge collection of tapes when he's on the road, people who "dis" (show disrespect for) Boston, prejudice, and war.

Did you know that Jon is not only the oldest New Kid, but he also has the biggest feet? He wears a size 10½! And were you aware that Jonathan used to be scared of the dark as a kid and that sometimes he sleeps with the bathroom light on?

Jon says his favorite memory is "spending time with my family at my grandparents' cottage in Canada." Jon is really down-to-earth! When road manager, Peter Work, called time-out and suggested that the Kids think up something mellow to do, Jon decided to go horseback riding! He's been fond of horses ever since he was little.

When asked what he looks for in a girl, this earthy New Kid's reply was: "Someone you can talk to and is

Though Jon has a reputation for being shy, he really loves to talk and has always been very popular. Larry Busacca/Retna

fun to be with—looks aren't everything.'' And if he had one wish, what would Jonathan wish for? For everyone to be happy, that's what! What a sweetheart!

3

JORDAN KNIGHT

HE'S COOL!

Jordan Knight describes himself as being the most "normal" guy in the group. What do the other guys think? Danny Wood describes Jordan as probably the most music-oriented of the New Kids. "He's really into playing the keyboards," says Danny. "He likes to be alone and think by himself." Donnie Wahlberg describes Jordan as being a real laid-back guy offstage. "Jordan is real smooth onstage—like glass," reveals Donnie.

Music is a huge part of Jordan's life. That's why even though the Kids had been touring for quite a while, when they had a few weeks off, Jordan chose to head straight for the studio and help out New Kids' opening act and good buddy, Tommy Page. Jordan first played the song "I'll Be Your Everything" for Tommy on a piano in a hotel lobby during the New Kids' Hangin' Tough tour. Tommy just about flipped out and told Jordan he got goosebumps from it! After the tour ended in September, Tommy, Jordan, Donnie and Danny worked on the music and polished up the lyrics. They also wrote and produced another tune with Tommy called "Turn On The Radio." Tommy released the

Jordan's plans for the future include producing records, writing new songs, or performing as a solo artist. Todd Kaplan, Star File

songs on his second album and "I'll Be Your Everything" went straight to the top of the charts!

Jordan is very talented—and also modest about his incredible talents! He's really big on honesty and gets to the point quickly. Jordan is an open-minded guy and doesn't like it when people judge others by their skin color or hair style.

It's Jordan's streak of uniqueness that makes him so very special. He gains great pleasure in helping others. He and Jon love their mother dearly. "She's the most important person in our lives," says Jordan. "Now we can repay some of the love she gave us."

Jordan really cherishes being close to his family. That's why he and Jonathan still live with their mom—sharing the whole "apartment" on the third floor.

Lately, Jordan has been spending his spare time at the gym. "I don't overdo it though—I'm not trying to look muscle-bound," clarifies Jordan. He says that working out helps to keep his energy level high for putting on a knockout show for beloved New Kids' fans everywhere!

To keep up with the New Kids' hectic schedules, one thing's for sure—you have to be in tiptop shape! Jordan keeps fit and healthy by working out and doing vigorous dance routines. And he makes a point of taking all of his vitamins each and every day! It's especially important that each of the New Kids eat balanced and nutritious meals because they need a lot of energy to perform. Jordan says that he doesn't gain weight when he's on the road with the Kids. "I lose three or four pounds in a couple of hours running around onstage," says Jordan.

In order to pump himself up for a show, Jordan and the Kids do wild 'n' crazy things. For instance, if you've ever been backstage right before a New Kids' show, you may have seen Jordan gearing up by doing some classic Michael Jackson moves. Sometimes, Jordan will walk around crooning Michael J. tunes, too! Once, some of the Kids hopped on some mopeds and whizzed by unsuspecting fans in a stadium parking lot only minutes before showtime. They made it onstage just in time!

Sometimes the Kids will wear disguises in order to mingle in a crowd. Donnie and Danny have dressed up like a wacky couple and strolled through hordes of their fans unnoticed. Jordan recalls another famous— but not so successful—instance when the Kids went masquerading in a Cleveland amusement park. "We went to the hot dog vendors and told them we needed their outfits and put them on—and I grabbed a broom," remembers Jordan with a chuckle. "We started walking through the park like we were selling hot dogs! It worked for about a second—but just for a second!"

While the New Kids are on the road, Jordan and Jon travel in their own tour bus and Danny, Joe and Donnie in another one. To unwind, Jordan and the other New Kids like to read, talk, eat, play Nintendo, play pranks on each other and, most importantly, sleep! Sometimes, Jordan will listen to some music. His musical tastes change rapidly. One minute he'll be listening to jazz and in the next, he'll be listening to the rap of Public Enemy. "I usually get into different phases," he says. "Sometimes for a month, I'll listen to mostly oldies and for the next, I'll listen to jazz and then rap. My music changes with my moods."

FAMILY
AND
FRIENDS

Jordan has said on many occasions how much he and Jonathan owe their family for the support they gave them when they decided to join the New Kids On The Block. Jordan is grateful not only for all the times the family watched the guys rehearse in the Knights' basement, but also for going to all those early gigs when the New Kids weren't so popular.

In addition to supporting the band as it was growing over the years, Marlene and the other Kids' mothers got together and formed the New Kids On The Block Fan Club. Early on, the moms used to run every aspect of the club. Now, they get a huge helping hand from their other children. Jon and Jordan's sisters, Sharon and Allison, work regularly at the fan club, sorting through the heaps of mail that the Kids get every day. Donnie's, Danny's and Joe's sisters and brothers also help to organize the fan mail.

Back when the band was just getting popular, the Kids would collect a lot of the plush toys that warm-hearted fans threw onstage or sent them from all over the world. "We've got cases full of them," says Jonathan. "I've got about 5000 teddy bears at home in my closet!" Now, although they keep many of the gifts fans send them, the Kids like to periodically donate some of the T−shirts and stuffed animals to children's hospitals and boys' clubs in the Boston area. The New Kids are just so generous and kind!

When a teen magazine asked Jon how he felt about having Jordan in the band with him, Jonathan replied, "It's the best! It's just so great. I mean we're all a close family, but there are just some things you can't tell

Jon and Jordan were too upbeat and determined to be discouraged by the failure of the New Kids' first album. Ernie Paniccioli

your closest friend that you can tell somebody who shares the same blood as you.''

All of the Kids are extremely proud of the New Kids On The Block's message. They're a positive group who encourage kids to be individuals and to strive to reach their dreams. Jordan and the rest of the Kids take every opportunity to tell kids it's cool to say ''no'' if you don't want to do something, whatever that may be—drugs, drinking, stealing, etc. It's important to be yourself. Jordan is very grateful that they were able to resist the bad influences of a fairly tough inner-city neighborhood. ''If we can survive, you can *definitely* survive,'' says Jordan.

THE
REAL
JORDAN

Jordan Knight likes to spend some of his spare time by himself. He loves to dance and he's constantly trying out new routines. He's a really energetic guy! His favorite book is *Jonathan Livingston Seagull,* and his fave play is *Julius Caesar* by William Shakespeare. His fave musicians are Maurice Starr, Prince, and Teddy Riley. And his fave song is "You Make Me Feel Brand New," by the Stylistics.

Some of the things on Jordan's "like" list are: basketball, the TV show *America's Most Wanted,* swimming, keyboards, Porsches, the color blue, Hawaii, actor Robert DeNiro, going to the beach, lasagna, chocolate milkshakes, and shopping for hip street clothes. Jordan also likes to go out on a cold morning, and he feels being on "a secluded beach at night with a fire" is the perfect way to spend an evening. As far as what he looks for in a girl, Jordan describes his perfect date as being "understanding, sweet and charming."

Some things on Jordan's "dislike" list are: prejudice, people who call the New Kids a "teenybopper group," bad comedy movies (he thinks all Eddie Murphy flicks are hilarious), and getting lost from the other guys in a foreign town.

Jordan loves to sing! In fact, his favorite childhood memory is "singing in the church choir." If he had one wish, what would Jordan wish for? "For there to be peace in the world." Great answer, Jordan!

Did you know that Jordan collects hotel room keys? How about that he's left-handed and he likes to put ketchup on everything? What about Jordan's secret dream? "My secret dream is to be in a movie with Eddie Murphy,'' reveals Jordan. And how about that Jordan is a really handsome and swell guy? Bet you already knew that!

It's a long way from William Monroe Trotter elementary school!
Janet Macoska

4

WHAT'S UP, KIDS?

STEP
BY
STEP

The New Kids On The Block climbed to the top step-by-step! Their fourth album, *Step By Step,* is rocking the charts and New Kids fever is rocking the world! Producer Maurice Starr says that *Step By Step* is the New Kids' "career album." By that he means that this will be the album that people will pick up thirty years from now when they want to hear something of the Kids' from way back when. *Step By Step* was mostly recorded in the various hotel rooms across America when the band was touring. "The reverb you can get from a hotel bathroom for the vocals—wow!" exclaims Maurice. "It's amazing!" If you've been looking for *Step By Step* on vinyl, look no further. This is the first album that the Kids released only in cassette and CD formats.

After wrapping up their Magic Summer '90 tour, the Kids will take a break and then head to Los Angeles. "We have the months of October, November and December blocked off our calendars because that's when we're going back to L.A. to film our movie," reveals Jonathan. The New Kids' cartoon, scheduled for this fall '90, should also be a real spectacular treat!

Meanwhile, New Kids On The Block dolls hit the stores in summer '90 and Hasbro Toys is predicting a difficult time keeping up with the demands for them. Also available are New Kids On The Block stage play-sets, telephones, microphones, cassette players with headphones, AM/FM radios and poster puzzles! Remember, Christmas is just around the corner!

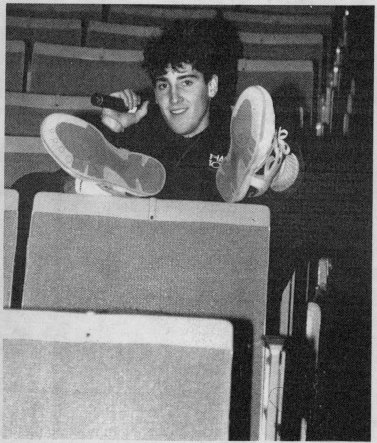

Jon has set aside his original plan to become an architect, and is thinking about managing a band of his own in the future. Ernie Paniccioli

Joe, Jordan, Danny, Donnie, and Jon definitely have the "right stuff."
Ernie Paniccioli

KIDS' STUFF

The New Kids may be called the "five hardest working kids in show business," but that doesn't mean they don't have time for plain old fun and games! Onstage, Donnie will pick up Jordan and pretend to throw him into the crowd. And any New Kids' opening act can attest to the fact that those New Kids are full of surprises! Once, they squirted Tommy Page with water guns when he was singing; they held the Cover Girls' feet from under the stage so they couldn't dance; and they taped the microphones to their stands so the girls from Sweet Sensation couldn't remove them!

If you've ever heard the name "J" and were wondering where it came from, then check this out! The Kids have the habit of making up all sorts of nicknames for each other. Danny is also known as "Puff McCloud;" Donnie's nickname is "Cheese;" Joe is "Bird;" Jonathan is "Jizz;" and Jordan is "J." Perfect Gentlemen's Tyrone Sutton says that Jordan is always making up all kinds of names for everybody. "Jordan is always giving people names like G and Z," says Tyrone, laughing. "He'll say 'You're X' and from then on that person will be X. Everyone will be like 'What's up, X?'" When asked about his nicknames, Jonathan exclaimed, "I have 10,000!"

Thinking up nicknames is not where the New Kids' creativity stops. They have also popularized a lot of street vocabulary. If something is "dope," it means it was excellent. He's "jive" means that he's a cool guy and he's hip. It's "hype" means it's great. It's "chillin'" and "fresh" mean it's good, cool and hot. Get it? Word!

Since the New Kids were formed over six years ago, they have accomplished so much, and have inspired so many. Their honesty, clean-cut image, and participation in organizations such as the Governor's Alliance Against Drugs prompted Governor Michael Dukakis of Massachusetts to declare every April 24 "New Kids On The Block Day!" Even the Beatles didn't get such an honor!

Over the years, Jon, Jordan, Donnie, Joe and Danny have grown very close. They really love being a part of New Kids On The Block because their fans make it very magical for them. When they're performing on stage, they're happy because they know they're making their fans happy. When they think about how far they've come, they never fail to appreciate their fans, families, Maurice, Mary Alford and all the others who supported them along the way.

As far as Jon's and Jordan's futures go, both feel that they will definitely stick with the New Kids as long as they still have gas. After that, they'll move on, but stay within the music field. Jon is thinking about moving into the business aspect of music, while Jordan may continue singing. Jon says that he thinks he'll get married someday, but that it's a long, long way off into the future. "I wouldn't mind getting married in eight to ten years—after I'm off the road," muses Jon.

Who can predict the future? Maurice Starr thinks that the New Kids On The Block may very well be around twenty or thirty years from now! You never know! In the meantime, all of the Kids are doing what they do best—performing and making great music for people everywhere.

"We'd like to say thank you to all of our fans for giving us the support we need—we love all our fans!" expresses Jordan. "The New Kids will be there for you all the time."

VITAL STATS

FULL NAME: Jonathan Rashleigh Knight
BIRTHDATE: November 29, 1968
EYE COLOR: Hazel
HAIR COLOR: Brown
HEIGHT: 5'11"
WEIGHT: 155 Lbs.
CURRENT RESIDENCE: Boston, Massachusetts
FAVE TYPE OF GAL: "Someone you can talk to and who is fun to be with!"

Larry Busacca/Retna Ltd.

Larry Busacca/Retna Ltd.

FULL NAME: Jordan Nathaniel Marcel Knight
BIRTHDATE: May 17, 1970
EYE COLOR: Brown
HAIR COLOR: Dark Brown
HEIGHT: 5′10″
WEIGHT: 155 Lbs.
CURRENT RESIDENCE: Boston, Massachusetts
FAVE TYPE OF GAL: "Understanding, sweet and charming!"

MUSIC AND VIDEOS

New Kids On The Block (Columbia, April 1986; Re-released 1989)

Tracks: "Stop It Girl" (M. Starr); "Didn't I (Blow Your Mind)?" (W. Hart, T. Bell); "Popsicle" (M. Starr); "Angel" (M. Starr, J. Cappra); "Be My Girl" (M. Starr); "New Kids On The Block" (M. Starr, D. Wahlberg); "Are You Down?" (AJ, E. Nuri, K. Banks, D. Wahlberg); "I Wanna Be Loved By You" (M. Starr); "Don't Give Up On Me" (M. Starr); "Treat Me Right" (M. Starr).

Hangin' Tough (Columbia, March 1988)

Tracks: "You Got It (The Right Stuff)" (M. Starr); "Please Don't Go Girl" (M. Starr); "I Need You" (M. Starr); "I'll Be Loving You (Forever)" (M. Starr); "Cover Girl" (M. Starr); "I Need You" (M. Starr); "Hangin' Tough" (M. Starr); "I Remember When" (M. Starr, E. Kelly, J. Randolph, C. Williams); "What'cha Gonna Do (About It)" (M. Starr); "My Favorite Girl" (M. Starr, D. Wahlberg, J. Knight); "Hold On" (M. Starr).

Merry, Merry Christmas (Columbia, September 1989)

Tracks: "This One's For The Children" (M. Starr); "Last Night I Saw Santa Claus" (M. Starr, A. Lancellotti); "I'll Be Missin' You Come Christmas (A Letter To Santa)" (K. Nolan, M. Starr); "I Still Believe In Santa Claus" (M. Starr, A. Lancellotti); "Merry, Merry Christmas" (M. Starr, A. Lancellotti); "The Christmas Song (Chestnuts Roasting On An Open Fire)" (M. Torme, R. Wells); "Funky, Funky Xmas" (M. Starr, D. Wahlberg); "White Christmas" (I. Berlin); "Little Drummer Boy" (K.K. Davis, B. Onorati, H. Simeone, adaptation by J. Edwards); "This One's For The Children" (Reprise).

Step By Step (Columbia, June 1990)

Tracks: Side One: "Step By Step" (M. Starr); "Tonight" (M. Starr, A. Lancellotti); "Baby, I Believe In You" (M. Starr); "Call It What You Want" (M. Starr); "Let's Try It Again" (M. Starr); "Happy Birthday" (M. Starr, M. Jonzun).

Side Two: "Games" (M. Starr, D. Wahlberg); "Time Is On Our Side" (M. Starr, A. Lancellotti); "Where Do We Go From Here?" (M. Starr); "Stay With Me, Baby" (M. Starr, M. Jonzun); "Funny Feeling" (M. Starr, M. Jonzun); "Never Gonna Fall In Love Again" (M. Starr, M. Jonzun, D. Wood).

Singles: "Step By Step" released 5/90; future singles not announced at press time.

SINGLES

"Be My Girl"
"Stop It Girl"
"Didn't I (Blow Your Mind)?"
"Please Don't Go Girl"
"You Got It (The Right Stuff)"
"I'll Be Loving You (Forever)"
"Cover Girl"
"Hangin' Tough"
"This One's For The Children"
"Step By Step"

MUSIC VIDEOS

"Please Don't Go Girl"
"You Got It (The Right Stuff)"
"I'll Be Loving You (Forever)"
"Cover Girl"
"Didn't I (Blow Your Mind)?"
"Hangin' Tough"
"This One's For The Children"
"Step By Step"

VIDEOCASSETTES

HANGIN' TOUGH (CBS Home Video, 1989)
This 30-minute home video contains interviews and backstage footage as well as videos for the four hits off the *Hangin' Tough* LP: "Please Don't Go Girl," "You Got It (The Right Stuff)," "I'll Be Loving You (Forever)" and "Hangin' Tough."

HANGIN' TOUGH LIVE (CBS Home Video, 1989)
Every New Kids' hit off their second LP is performed live in this half-hour-long cassette.

AWARDS AND HONORS

AMERICAN MUSIC AWARDS
—Favorite Pop/Rock Album (*Hangin' Tough*)
—Favorite Pop/Rock Group

BOSTON MUSIC AWARDS
—Outstanding Pop/Rock Single ("I'll Be Loving You Forever")
—Outstanding Video ("Hangin' Tough")
—Act Of The Year

GRAMMY NOMINATION
—Best Music Video (Long Form)

ON TOUR

European and Magic Summer Tour Photos

Meyer/Fotex/Shooting Star

Meyer/Fotex/Shooting Star